EXPO
SURE

war
media
democracy

Hatred, division, and lack of respect
arise from a failure of imagination.

Colm Tóibín

To a wonderful former colleague in the business of culture.
Angela.

poems

Angela Graham

thanks & acknowledgements

It is a pleasure to thank the publisher, Phil Cope, once again, for his generous and unfailing encouragement and rigour. Poet, Julian Cason has been an insightful reader throughout this book's development. I appreciate the critical eye of Damian Smyth, Head of Literature at the Arts Council of Northern Ireland. An editorial appraisal by Natasha Cuddington of Macha Press was very helpful at an early stage, and Angeline King generously read a draft.

And thanks to the many poets, writers and readers who form the creative atmosphere that sustains my writing, and to Ballycastle Creative Writers Group and The Third Thursday Club for their friendship and support. I'm grateful to Ashley Todd for her insights into Ulster-Scots and to Elaine Gaston for her engagement with my poetry.

My husband, John Geraint and my son and daughters, Seán, Anwen and Róisín are always lovingly supportive and patient and make me laugh!

Several poems in this collection were first published in the following print and online journals: Abridged, Agenda (IWA), The Bangor Literary Journal, Crannóg, The Honest Ulsterman, Impspired, The Interpreter's House, NAWR, Pissoir, The Storms and New Isles Press journal; and in the anthologies Last Light: Apocalypse Poetry and High Rise (Broken Spine Books), We Not Me/Ni Nid Fi (Culture Matters) and Yarns (USCN). 'Opening Hell' was commissioned by Poetry Jukebox for the Linen Hall Library's Fragments of Scotch Poetry project 2025. 'The Transactionalist' was a runner-up in the Seamus Heaney Award for New Writing 2025 and published in the Community Arts Partnership anthology 2025.

The epigraph is from Colm Tóibín's 'Along the Catalan and Irish borders: Politics of memory and progress through imagination', address to the British-Irish Association's annual Conference, 2009 (reprinted in Journal of Cross Border Studies in Ireland, 2024).

COVER: my left iris, taken by Brian McKeown of www.irisphotographyni.co.uk.
The image 'Combat training soldiers 25 Airborne Brigade of the Armed Forces of Ukraine' by Taras Gren and Ministry of Defence of Ukraine, retrieved from https://w.wiki/H8Ch, is licensed under Creative Commons Attribution-Share Alike 2.0 Generic (https://. creativecommons.org/licenses/by-sa/2.0/deed.en). Accordingly, the cover image is licensed under the Creative Commons Attribution-Share Alike 2.0 Generic license (https://creativecommons.org/licenses/by-sa/2.0/deed.en).

ISBN: 978-1-0686946-2-2

a *culture & democracy press* publication
www.cultureanddemocracypress.co.uk
Facebook: https://tinyurl.com/CultureAndDemocracyPress

foreword

Images are everywhere. We respond to more and more of them every day of our lives. Our exposure to images affects our perceptions, our attitudes, our spirits. It's also a significant source of creative engagement with the world.

This book starts from a single photographic image. It was taken on the second day of a war and seen by me in the online edition of a newspaper on the war's first anniversary. Its impact was so strong that I allowed it to draw me into a consideration of how photographs, journalism, and other images communicate reality, in particular the reality of war and conflict, and how exposure to them affects my own inner 'reality'.

Through these media, the world 'out there' penetrates the 'in here' of the reader or viewer. Poetry does this too in its own way. Journalists and poets work with the image and the word.

The focus of the first section of the book: **Soldiers and Civilians** is on the Russian invasion of Ukraine and the Israel/Gaza war. The second section: **Politicians and Citizens** is about conflict in civil society.

This collection is in the tradition of photopoetry (a symbiosis of photographs and poems) but with the photographs deliberately left out. The poems stand on their own terms as expressions of my personal dialogue with these images and as speculation on their societal impact.

Some readers may want to see the images that gave rise to the poems. Several are behind paywalls but, where possible, I give references for access (as also for other media) and credit the relevant photographers, journalists and platforms. But my belief is that appreciation of the poems does not depend on seeing the photographs.

I spent decades as a documentary-maker and worked in feature film scripting and production, so I am not naïve about the process of the framing, editing and composition of images. I regard them as the raw material of my working life.

Imagination, our personal image system, is a powerful force. It can foster empathy or prejudice.

In many of the poems I speak in the voice of a version of someone I have met only through the media. This entering into another life through the door of the imagination is something I believe human beings do instinctively but not merely compulsively. We have some choice in the process. We make up dialogue, thoughts or actions, in our attempt to see the world through someone else's eyes, so the poems, though they are prompted by reality, are not strictly documentary in nature.

There is some Welsh, Irish and Ulster-Scots in the collection as these languages are part of my cultural experience.

I grew up in Northern Ireland during 'The Troubles'. When I was eleven, I saw, on the tv news, footage of establishment brutality being meted out; a brutality my community knew about but which had, until then, been kept hidden and denied. This was a tremendous catalyst for change. To see can become to witness; and it can go further, into bearing witness; into becoming a protagonist in the creation of truth, in word or action.

Exposure to challenging reality is painful but the potential of our personal agency, and of the ways in which we choose to respond, is central to the collection and to democracy.

Angela Graham

SOLDIERS AND CIVILIANS

THE RUSSIAN INVASION OF UKRAINE

PHOTOGRAPHS OF A DEAD RUSSIAN SOLDIER
ON THE OUTSKIRTS OF KHARKIV,
taken 24 – 27 February 2022

PHOTOGRAPH OF A DEAD RUSSIAN SOLDIER

taken 26 February 2022,
seen by me on the war's first anniversary

Rotting inside his uniform – he would be
but his final lover, the snow,
has lain on him so intimately
he is possessed entire;
his face veiled;
his right arm flung out on frozen linen
in his last abandon.

His up-turned wrist, his naked palm – florid – mimic life
but his fingers have scooped deep in a font of snow
as though he'll rise and bless himself, thumb a swift cross
on our foreheads, eyes, lips, hearts,
shudder, and stumble on.

He'll not be rising.
In a corner of the frame some pre-fab storage units
hint that he died in the back lot of a retail park.
Ochre and khaki, his stricken tank, behind him
(he did not leap far)
is motionless and only metal now.

I see the stillness, and the snow – a stalled assault,
already a year ago.

From all of this I can't wring any meaning.

Photo Credit:
Sergey Bobok / AFP / Getty Images 1238775404, 26 February 2022.
Source: *The Atlantic* 'Photos: Chaos and Resistance in Ukraine'
by Alan Taylor, 27 February 2022
https://www.theatlantic.com/photos-chaos-and-resistance-ukraine/622947/7

PHOTOGRAPH OF A DEAD RUSSIAN SOLDIER: SHIFTED POINT OF VIEW

Newly framed
– further shamed –
he lies dead
by a road.
Slick tarmac
army track;
human sack
slung off-road.

Photo Credit: Unsourced

BOTH PHOTOGRAPHS

In winter, when I was very young, I'd find
the inside of my bedroom window slicked with ice, opaque'd.
I'd stand close up to scrutinise that alien terrain,
its glistening battlements and outposts,
not knowing that the tiny engine of my breath
was sapping it, until, with a sudden bloom,
the glass would clear and I'd be looking through
to the other side.

In the aftermath of snow, the air is numb.

I've lived with these two photographs,
returning to re-see, reflect and –
realise I'm looking at myself:
I, lying on the hard, wet ground;
I, framing, and shifting the vantage-point;
I, who shoot / am shot.

In the aftermath of snow, the air is clear.

The photographer and I at once distinct
and consubstantial; the photographed
and I – yes, the same applies.
Then / now; there / here –
I have been, suddenly, let through.
Does this amount to meaning?

In the aftermath of snow, the air bristles, and breathes.

FINDING AN EARLIER SHOT
taken 24 February 2022

Today I found another shot of that tank
and the dead Russian but no snow.
The sun is pulling the last of its orange self
down behind the wholesale sheds
while grey clouds crowd the brilliant backwash.

It's skid-marked asphalt that he lies on
in his green camouflage. He has a face.
The superstructure of the tank is pink.
Beyond it are the tops of giant letters R K I V
in turquoise and yellow.

Day one of this particular invasion
and Maksim Levin photographs
spent matériel, and one spent life
that nobody had time to focus on.
Which is why he does.

When later photographers arrived,
the day or two gone by
had closed the sky down,
drained the colour out, brought
at least the ministrations of snow.

Photo Credit: Maksim Levin / Reuters, 24 February 2022
'R K I V': from the word 'KHARKIV'.
In situ these letters appear in the Cyrillic alphabet as 'Р К І В'.

'tank' – later I understood the vehicle was an APC, an armoured personnel carrier

MAKSIM LEVIN'S CREDO

Every Ukrainian photographer
dreams of taking a photo
that will stop the war.

We know we're reachable
through what we see
but nowhere have I found such faith

that this particular art
can nerve us to feel
and judge aright.

Three weeks in,
Maksim Levin
was caught and killed.

He was in a hurry,
a colleague says, *to find truth,*
the first victim of wars.

First Quotation: Maksim Levin
Second Quotation: Patrick Chauvel, co-author of the investigation by Reporters Without Borders into the death of Maksim Levin
https://rsf.org/en/exclusive-investigation-death-maks-levin-information-and-evidence-collected-indicates

PROOF IN THE FORM OF IMAGES

Maksim Levin died in the forest near Huta-Mezhyhirs'ka
in the effort to retrieve his drone and its photographs,
in the effort to retrieve proof in the form of images.

Reporters Without Borders
can hypothesise the sequence of events
but there is no proof in the form of images.

Oleksiy Chernyshov, the soldier who was with him,
was shot and burned. His charred remains, bullets,
detritus and Levin's corpse offer forensic evidence

but no proof in the form of images
of that ambush, interrogation, execution
apart from those developing in your mind.

Title: Patrick Chauvel, co-author of investigation by Reporters Without Borders into the death of Maksim Levin: 'Maksim Levin died in the forest near Huta-Mezhyhirs'ka in the effort to retrieve his drone and its photographs, in the effort to retrieve proof in the form of images.'

AN ACT OF MERCY?

taken 25 February 2022

Snow is indiscriminate
... on flesh, on steel ...
it's we who read intention
into its accumulations.

It reached Kharkiv at half-past eight
on this invasion's second day.
I claim it had asperged and set apart
the parking lot on the northern ring road
by the time that Tyler Hicks,
doyen of war photographers, arrived.

He foregrounds the splayed corpse;
in parallel, the emptied APC;
a perfect fan of emptied winter branches
by the top left corner
gives a sense of distance and proportion

so, on *The New York Times* front page
next day at breakfast time, death and defeat,
bloodless, poignantly veiled.

Other photographers
render these circumstances
but here the top of frame is cropped
before it can reveal this Russian died
at the stanchion of a sign assuring him
RST-КУПИТИ АВТО
Best Place To Buy A Car.

Photo Credit: Tyler Hicks / *The New York Times*, 25 February 2022
Source: *The New York Times*, 26 February 2022
Also https://www.gettyimages.co.uk/detail/news-photo/the-front-page-of-the-new-york-times-shows-a-picture-of-a-news-photo/1373108497

LOWER ANGLE

taken 25 February 2022

This photographer steps left, crouches a little,
frames the dead Russian
as the head of a recessional
slanting rightward across the frame
– the burnt-out APC, spent armoured truck,
those lumpen hangars –
under a sky like a leaden coffer lid

but that barely settled snow
is the held
breath
after a nightmare,
the heart – panicked –
trying to escape the body
in a runnel of its own blood.

Photo Credit: Sergey Kozlov / EPA 25 February 2022.
Photo of the Year, Istanbul Photo Awards 2023

REVERSED POINT OF VIEW

taken 25 February 2022

Kozlov comes at things a different way:
foregrounds the APC,
notes the corpse on its far side
but gives us
– beyond a flimsy palisade of naked trees –
the whiteness,
always biding its time.

Photo Credit: Sergey Kozlov / EPA, 25 February 2022

WEATHER

The snowfall turned to a grim miasma
in which the vast steppe cloaked itself,
bearing down on this roadside clearing
by the outsize letters of the city's name
where soldiers, facing east, huddled to confront
whatever would come lumbering out of the mist.

Dead man, dead vehicles – undisturbed,
until the cold unclenches
and Sergey Bobok takes the photograph
that was the first I saw, patches of camouflage
emerging like moss
in a parody of Spring.

1st stanza Photo Credit: Maksim Levin / Reuters, 25 February 2022
2nd stanza Photo Credit: Sergey Bobok /AFP / Getty Images, 26 February 2022
Source: *The Atlantic* 'Photos: Chaos and Resistance in Ukraine' by Alan Taylor, 27th February 2022
https://www.theatlantic.com/photo/2022/02/photos-chaos-and-resistance-ukraine/622947/#img03

MOVING ON

possibly taken 26 February 2022

We glimpse the adjacent ring road
where hoardings like triumphal standards
process to a vanishing point
– something being laughingly consumed.

Photographer: Uncredited
Source: Ukrinform https://www.ukrinform.net
rubric-ato/3960854-russias-war-casualty-toll-in-ukraine-up-1530-over-past-day.html

VISITANTS

taken 27 February 2022

By now, thick slush hides blood.
Photographers leave themselves
in each other's images:
melt-water puddles of their footprints
– tracks of their search for points of view –
traces of their taking and moving on

so I can walk as they did, past the body
by the head, around the rear of the APC,
return to the Russian in the henge
raised by our boot-prints; look at him,
in his sacred circle of uninvaded snow,
and leave him there because he's dead.

Once I step out of that frame
of arrested time, it becomes a pool
that I look into but it's I
who ripple, shivered by currents, stirred
and questioning, and
still alive.

Photo Credit: Jack Crosbie
Source: *Rolling Stone*, 2 March 2022, 'Fleeing Kharkiv, Leaving Death and Destruction Behind in Ukraine' by Jack Crosbie

EXPOSURE

a photograph is a theatre
a place for seeing things

we look
though we can never intervene

no outcry, no appeal
can change the fact

in pain's front line someone
has suffered unchangeably.

Like that half-dead man
on the road to Jericho

the photograph, unmoving,
moves us

– viscerally –
to implicate ourselves,

to feel
as a stranger felt,

to be
beyond ourselves.

Greek θέατρον, théatron: a place for seeing, from θεάομαι, theáomai: to see or observe

THE RUSSIAN INVASION OF UKRAINE

I IMAGINE BEING

ON PRESUMING TO SPEAK IN THE PERSONA OF SOMEONE ENCOUNTERED THROUGH JOURNALISM

A bridge is a leap
– a bow bent –
a thing committed to
from the first step

and good reportage
like an arrow nocked
or a bridge embarked on
is momentum

that carries you
even
beyond yourself
even

into a life
not yours
you are delivered
and when

you retrieve
yourself
you know
you've been changed

and something
of someone else's life
can speak
through you

changed
yes
but itself
in you

like a seed lodged
flowering
with unexpected
petals

facts and imagination
crossing the gap
like a bridge
like an arrow

I IMAGINE BEING A UKRAINIAN SOLDIER, WHO SPEAKS TO ME FROM INSIDE THE BESEIGED AZOVSTAL STEELWORKS
Mariupol

I watched you coming down the steps of your imagination
to join us in this last makeshift redoubt. Yes, all the infantry
of the 36th brigade are dead and so few of us marines are left
that our cooks are now artillerymen; the messroom waiters
ferry ammunition; the radio operators, orderlies and drivers,
the storemen, even the regimental band – all in the frontline now.

A local postman barrelled in beside me, clutching a gun
and his last armful of undelivered mail.
At night he sorts it carefully into piles, crooning the names
of Mariupol streets that have been pulverised.
He's magicking an after-all-this time when there'll be letterboxes,
bills and greeting cards. We expect to die. A day. Or two.

That hand among the rubble? Dmytro. Something in him snapped.
He swore he would out-scream the Russian shells. He wouldn't stop
so I had to knock him out. The silence afterwards was worse because
it had nothing human in it. When we had to move,
I said to leave him be. *He'll catch us up. Pity to bring him round.*
Then I saw his eyelids open just as a slab of ceiling fell ...

We're told we ought to pray for souls who put one foot across the threshold
into death and hover, undecided. He had no time to waver.
And why should any of us hope for a merciful escape? God only had one son
and didn't spare him.
It will be Easter soon.
Because that roof-fall blocked our exit, this is our tomb.
Come down those stairs tomorrow, and the next day.
It helps – I admit – to think we're not alone.

Sources: *The Guardian*, 12 April 2022, "Last marines defending Mariupol now 'running out of ammunition'" by Luke Harding, Bethan McKernan, Isobel Koshiw; and video on Facebook of Serhiy Volyna,(Serhii Volynskyi), Commander, 36th Marine Brigade, 20 April 2022
https://www.facebook.com/100009516031304/videos/519753423058534/

The soldier in the poem is fictional.
The Russian siege of Mariupol lasted from 24 February to 20 May 2022. The Azovstal steel works was the last site of major resistance by Ukrainian forces. Many civilians took refuge there.

I IMAGINE BEING OLEH BONDARENKO
Motyzhyn

I thought of it as a solemn thing;
a science, even, carefully applied for maximum effect
and, yes, the veterans of the Syria Campaign are masters of routine.
They torture by the book, with flair.
To them, our village is a fairyland compared to where they've been:
plenty to eat, to steal, to drink and we share a language,
so no tedious pantomiming what they mean to do:
they can add to our torment with a casual word.

They made me run towards Death – blindfolded, bullets at my heels –
then pushed Him away, laughing, telling me to try again, but harder,
as they tied me to a quad bike and swore that if I fell,
as it swerved and juddered, there'd be no mercy.
A bombardment started and they left me
tied me up in the open as they ran for cover:
Let your own kill you. A day, a night, another day and night ...
my blood stumbling and faltering in my collapsing veins.

I could hear them killing someone, slowly.
So very slowly that I prayed he'd die.
I wondered, dazedly, had I become more merciful than God?
When they finished him, they drank, strutting on corpses,
boasting of what they'd done in Syria and how losers everywhere
deserved far worse than they ever got. Still, tomorrow,
there'd be another chance to raise their game.
Then, suddenly, I was lifted.

I was carried to a corner of some room, laid on the dirty floor
by Russian soldiers – but regular recruits. They said the commanders
would assume that I'd been dumped with the other dead.
Two days later they returned. They were moving out.
They asked me to pray for them. They who were fighting
to stay human in the midst of hell ...
To this day I pray ....
They saved my life.

Source: *The Observer*, 1 May 2022, 'How the barbaric lessons learned in Syria came to haunt one small, faraway village'
Journalists: Emma Graham-Harrison, Isobel Koshiw, Lorenzo Tondo

Words in italics are from the report.

I IMAGINE BEING VOVAN, UNIT COMMANDER IN THE DEFENCE OF KHARKHIV

November/December 2023

When I made it back home, Mama cried out,
My golden boy! My little fish!,
bending my head down to hers,
kissing my hair, eyes, forehead,
and I swam in the dam-burst of love
that swept through our apartment,
all of them hugging, stroking,
holding onto me as though amazed
I was flesh and blood, not a ghost
returned from that savage borderland.
I say, and I don't say, what I did there.

Source: BBC 2 documentary, 'Ukraine: Enemy In The Woods',
Hoyo Films. First broadcast, 25 March 2024
BAFTA for Best Single Documentary 2025

Words in italics are from the film.

I IMAGINE BEING VOVAN, ON FURLOUGH

At night I watch the lights from traffic at the intersection
chase each other across the ceiling
– shadows writing ...
They swing in urgent arcs, or float and fade
– such anxious angels.
Or maybe the roof is perforated, letting strange lights through.
I can't get a fix on what's outside, or in.
I lose perspective and proportion.
I lost myself today among the supermarket aisles.

Sleep is a shallow dug-out where I dream a cathedral
of so many pillars there's no room to pray,
and they refuse to form a line, no aisles:
move and these trees move with you.
Between slender saplings I am a bottom-feeder,
darting over an ocean floor of snow, chasing shadows
and never any sky or sunlight, just dawn/day/twilight/night ...
I wake, and, overhead, angels and drones ...
I have a feeling that the forest will never leave me.

Source: BBC 2 The documentary 'Ukraine: Enemy In The Woods',
Hoyo Films. First broadcast, 25 March 2024.
BAFTA for Best Single Documentary 2025

Words in italics are from the film

MAKING CONTACT, MARCH 2025

During a Russian tank attack ten months ago
Vovan was suddenly let through.
He is where I am not – yet –
Time will deliver me.

The dead are reticent. No need to cajole
or threaten us. We will arrive.
Time will deliver us
– each of us suddenly let through.

Here, via sound and shadow in a film,
something of Vovan entered me, to stay.
There, he and I will be suddenly let through
to one another ... suddenly let through

Vovan died in the spring of 2024.

THE RUSSIAN INVASION OF UKRAINE

IMAGE

A MATTER OF DEGREE

Bucha, Suburban Kyiv

A naked woman in a fur coat, dead.
Condom wrappers on the floor above.
What happened there – it wasn't love.
Scant radio news, but in my head
these words kept pressing to be understood
– something to grasp here, if I could.

The condom-users gone, a woman dead.
But why in fur? A pornographic hook?
She wanted it so much she chose this look:
deluxe seduction, high-class come-to-bed.
Is that the fantasy they made her play:
the lustful woman leading men astray?

woman in fur coat condoms dead
One click: *The New York Times.* She lay,
prone on a blanket, on backyard clay.
A short fur jacket pulled up to her head
conceals her face – her hair spread wide
like a dreaming débutante's. She died
in the cellar under the garden shed.
Long skid marks on her livid thighs
show she'd been dragged out. I realise
the photographer has given her a shred
of dignity: she's naked from the waist
but a passing policeman blocks our gaze.

As my small mercy I will leave unsaid
the detail of her extreme exposure
to the men who, as they shot her, posed her
so we'd know she was, to them, degraded.
Then they withdrew. Tower blocks look down
on the wire netting of the chicken run
where Mr Shepitko's trees spread
their bare branches over his smallholding
and the gloved young man focused on unfolding
a green/pink chevroned cover for a bed
and the policeman stooping by her head
and the old buckets, ash heaps and that shed.

A naked woman in a fur coat, dead.
Those soldiers – they buried themselves in her.
Contempt, I see, is at the root of murder.
I search my conscience and I count my dead.

Sources: BBC Radio 4, *The World At One*, 5 April 2022
Photo Credit: Daniel Berehulak
The New York Times, 11 April 2022, 'Bucha's Month of Terror'
by Carlotta Gall

PHOTOGRAPH OF A YOUNG MAN IN A HOODIE
Kyiv

Yes, it haunts me – his kneeling body pleated tight,
head in his hands,

a hooded monk – but worship
doesn't call for such extreme prostration,

his palms a second cranium
now all other shelter's gone.

This is what love looks like
when the beloved has been snatched away

by shrapnel
and there's been time enough

only for someone to find something
in this carpark to throw over her

– that gesture of goodbye
once the border's crossed.

Photo credit: Fadel Senna / AFP, taken in Kyiv 17 March 2022
Caption: 'A desperate inhabitant of Kyiv near a wrapped body after debris of a downed rocket hit a residential building, on March 17, 2022'
Source: AFP correspondent blog, Agence France-Presse: 'Ukraine: When Things Fall Apart'
Contributing testimonies: Dave Clark, Sophie Estienne, Dmytro Gorshkov, Antoine Lambroschini, Karim Menasria, Daphné Rousseau, Olga Shylenko, Arman Soldin, Daniel Leal
Interviews by Michaëla Cancela-Kieffer in Paris /
English version by Fiachra Gibbons
https://correspondent.afp.com/ukraine-when-things-fall-apart

YOUR WORST FEAR

photograph of a dead Russian soldier on a road,
Makarivka

He has been left as a message
pasted on the tarmac,
a handbill of the thinnest paper
– his flattened uniform and helmet –
but for one rubber boot sole,
crushed, and crushed, re-crushed
– a pop-up that doesn't understand it's dead;
his foot caught by a caterpillar track
powering up heel, shin, thigh, hip, rib perhaps
his mind blew up
before his skull exploded.

No, they wouldn't stop to save him
nor you.
War is a generalist
so be particular,
re-compose him in a poem
– not as God would,
re-uniting flesh and essence –
but in that last sprint
before the bullet spun him.
Take time, then, to scrape yourself
up off the ground.

Photo Credit: Tyler Hicks, taken on 26 July 2023
Sources: *The New York Times* '2023 The Year in Pictures'
AI-AP American Photography 40 Winners 2023
https://www.ai-ap.com/slideshow/AP/40/tyler-hicks/

PRIGOZHIN'S SLAVES

A staple of the sword-and-sandals epic, the galley slave,
powering some trireme at the empire's will,
is a hollow choice embodied: labour or die; die labouring.

Those Russian convicts who were made to choose
either to fight with Wagner or stay jailed
– freedom to fight and, fighting, die –

can we call them mercenaries? Their pay is docked
by death. Then they're framed for camera
in cynically tragic terms: *Fighters for Freedom.*

Traitors or patriots, what twisting of the flesh and mind
powered those feet heading for Moscow,
then turned round – bidden / re-bidden slaves?

The days of barbarism, mustering on the hilltop
as they always do, wait for us to signal that we want them
now; want them to swoop – harsh problem solvers –

because we always want them
or we would have penned such obscene choices
in the past.

Yevgeny Prigozhin, a Russian oligarch, led the private military company, the Wagner group, funded by the Russian state and active in Syria, Russia and Ukraine. On 23 June 2023, he rebelled against Russian leadership and launched an advance on Moscow. The following day, he called off the rebellion and agreed with the Russian state to relocate his forces to Belarus.

Source: *The Guardian*, 20 September 2022
Article Credit: Pjotr Sauer, 'We thieves and killers are now fighting Russia's war: how Moscow recruits from its prisons. Inmates describe visits by Yevgeny Prigozhin ... who is said to offer pardons for those who enlist.'
Image Credit: Twitter

INFLATION

Yevgeny Prigozhin b. 1961

If it's true he exploded in mid-air,
what end more fitting?
He was always on the up.
A petty criminal who felt himself grow big
through the feeding of unspeakable desires,
tonguing deep.
And how easy it all was!
From the Donbas a step to Syria;
to Africa a stride;
a pivot to Ukraine
and where next then
but the Motherland,
the ultimate, the incestuous, assault.
We all know he withdrew,
and where then only up
and up
and

Yevgeny Prigozhin, Russian oligarch and leader of the private military company, the Wagner group, born 1961, died in a business jet crash on 23 August 2023 which was possibly caused by sabotage

TRUMP, VANCE, 28 February 2025

An evening when the sky is soft blue plumage,
from its height of indigo, where a star, or satellite,
grows brighter by the moment, to the downiest smudge
behind a charcoal frieze – the chimney pots and aerials –

while live on tv a righteous posse bays around Zelenskyy,
relishing the taunts before the kill,
showing us how a lynching's done,
with a-whoopin' an' a-hollerin'.

In what appalling cranny is their own humiliation stashed,
for only the deeply shamed can shame with so much relish?
And now we've seen how they mean to treat us all,
how they hope we'll treat each other – the weak culled –

we recall that flash-lit Nineteen-Thirty night in Indiana,
the White folks milling in a carnival mood,
a fierce little man with a Hitler 'tache
pointing to the Black men hanging from the tree.

Sources: BBC 1 News, 28 February 2025

A photograph by Lawrence Beitler, taken 7 August 1930
in Marion, Indiana, shortly after the lynching of Thomas Shipp
and Abraham Smith in front of a crowd of 5,000

I IMAGINE THE WAR APPROACHES MY TOWN

Maria would stand looking out
from the height above the harbour
where the few remaining boats bridle and jostle
and the last ferry is leaving for the island.

Impossible to separate
the many greys of the sea
or to know exactly when that sac of clouds
will burst over the distant headland

but Maria is fit for anything
as she takes my arm
and I feel how firm
her grasp is.

Her eyes are so clear
that I know she has rinsed them in sorrow
and is sure she can meet it again
and be brave.

An army is coming
along the coast road.
Their drones will be ahead of them,
shredding the air

but Maria intends to be
clothed with the sun,
crowned with stars,
terrible as an army with banners.

She is pregnant
– most vulnerable,
most strong –
whereas they only know how to kill.

STATION FIFTEEN

Kryvyi Rih

Christ dies at the Thirteenth Station.
From the show trial of the First,
through the tortures, to the death,
we walk with him, as witnesses.

Moving along a path of images
– his crown of thorns ... his scourging ... each collapse –
we read his humiliation and his wounds
through the lens of our particular pain.

At the Fourteenth, his friends prise the nails
out of the feet, the hands,
and lumber the sagging bone-sack down
to the pointless cradle of his mother's arms.

I could place this woman and this soldier here
among the many attitudes of grief
but they belong where the last of hope is gone
– Station Fifteen.

Centre foreground she is kneeling,
palms raised, eyes shut.
He genuflects to her
(his right leg stiff and wounded).

The photographer must be kneeling too
for the low lens brings us all
to our knees
– Magi at an emptied crib.

The soldier (father?) bows his head
in homage to her wailing ...
The swings, the climbing-frame,
are piled with teddy bears and flowers.

A small boy, well-wrapped up,
nudges a cairn of soft toys with his foot
and posters of nine killed children
hang from the playground slide.

I can't make the Stations at the church this year
– my left foot broken and my right arm bust –
but I can follow, in the photojournalists' footsteps,
the Via Dolorosa of Ukraine.

Will I drown in such catastrophic images?
Not in these pools, composed, and deep;
repositories of the real,
as icons are.

Photo Credit: Evgeniy Maloletka / AP
Caption: 'Playground where a Russian rocket killed 9 children on Friday 4 April 2025 in Kryvyi Rih, Ukraine'
Source: *The Guardian*, 10 April 2025

DIALOGUE

In a pail of water I am looking up at myself looking down.
Does the water know?

The saint in the icon appears to return my gaze
but the painted pupil is a door, opening ....

Does the photograph return my scrutiny?
As a window reflects. I bring myself to what I see.

Whichever hunger dominates the heart
prompts the human gaze to flinch, devour or savour ...

The eye of the photographer knows this, invites
collusion – cruel, compassionate or joyful –

but always there are ripples it will never see, and can't control,
for the gaze hosts image upon image and,

even if the photographs are cached,
they are still, in your life and in mine, proliferating;

never neutral;
like a kiss from Christ or Judas.

THOUGH I AM NOT IN THE WAR ZONE

I am framed on the one loom
that is weaving me and plying
these threads of other lives
into and out of mine.

The photographer shows us
to ourselves through one another;
how we're each
as transient as a turned page.

'LET THE ATROCIOUS IMAGES HAUNT US.'

When a visitation happens,
I recognise the revenant
– a brother with an urgent message
and a mirror ...

I live among voices.

Sometimes, the crescendo of the harm
we do each other deafens me
and sometimes I say
its battering numbs my eyes ...

But that's my courage failing.

The image, dream or phantom
shows itself.
I must discern
whether to let it in.

How to act? It never tells me.

No image
will change the world.
We do that
or not.

Title: Susan Sontag, 'Regarding the Pain of Others'
(Farrar, Strauss and Giroux, 2003)

THE ISRAEL / GAZA WAR

IMAGINING

IMAGINING, IN THE UK

7 October 2023

I am beside myself. I watch myself at table, eating,
amazed the food isn't exploding
and the kitchen's where I left it.
I stand in the shoes of a man
immobile at a ruined hospital in Gaza,
my arms the aching cradle for my shattered son.
I am the soldier carapaced in body armour, helmet, visor,
telling the British journalist that, *No,*
until today I'd never seen
the lopped head of a child.

IN A BOMBARDED CITY

Do you think we're crazy people,
staunching a cracking dyke
while behind us there's an ocean pouring in?

As the paramedic loads the ambulance
his nape is scorched by the shock wave
from another missile strike.

We rush the wounded to the blasted hospital
as though the rituals of rescue conjure up
a theatre, anaesthetists.

This is normal we're performing
so the children will believe that here were streets
with flower sellers, pavement cafés ...

Our memory is their dream – their myth? –
though it was never more than fantasy
passing for peace.

In all those years of not-war,
our flimsy chairs were perched on glass
crazing over the abyss.

You, who watch us on your screens,
from your boulevards, your coffee-breaks,
look down ... look down at your feet.

BOMBARDED CITY 2

Three seconds ... for the apartment block
– its honeycomb of lives – to pleat down on itself
like a folding paper lantern.

I know, by now, not to run immediately forward
– shifts and settlements, groanings, sudden gasps,
as matter shuffles and re-shuffles itself.

I saw a paperclip (bent from office use)
slide down a concrete slab to a stop.
It looked exactly as before the missile struck.

I claimed it. My infinitesimal salvage. A talisman,
I wear it, knotted on a thread around my neck.
My heir, I tell it about everything that used to be.

I describe to it my mother's storage chest
– precious wedding clothes, and linens, veils, wadded tight
yet always she'd find room for one more thing.

It's a miracle so many horrors, relentlessly packed in,
can be accommodated – somewhere –
inside me.

My paperclip
– my touchstone of the ordinary, the routine –
later ... later you and I will rifle, discard, control.

BOMBARDED CITY 3

The air has changed. It shrinks from us when we emerge
– the sun a shrivelled leaf, the air thinning.
Even the ants limp and
the cats are eating their own paws.
Buildings lean on one another like exhausted beggars.
Salvage? An obscene dream.

This morning I wondered,
Is it time for me to hate myself?
Then I found a teenage boy,
sobbing
where there used to be a doorway.
I put my remaining arm around him.

I IMAGINE I AM NOOR'S MOTHER

Keep her above ground
for two more days.
Allah will understand.

Six years of marriage
before He gave her to me.
I was so happy.

In two more days
she would have been so happy
– a milestone in her little life,

to get that piece of paper.
In two more days
I'll cut a small slit in her shroud

and slip it in
– her school certificate.
Allah will understand.

Footage from Gaza City
with voiceover by Foreign Affairs Correspondent, Paraic O'Brien
Source: Channel 4 News, 22 September 2025

IMAGINATION

A woman told me that she never dreams,
never has a nightmare; that she blocks the bad things out;
that, *Atrocities? Well, we can't know, can we?*

I envied her untroubledness – briefly. Born into Ulster,
my whole life I've had to think about revenge:
what was taken; what should be taken back.

Vengefulness, like her, has tunnel vision,
whereas imagination
from its many watchtowers

dares to pick out mercy slowly getting to its feet
out on the battlefield, coming forward
through the dust clouds and shells.

THE ISRAEL / GAZA WAR

NEWS REACHES ME

OPENING HELL

President Trump and I ... have a common strategy ...
including when the gates of Hell will be opened ...
Benjamin Netanyahu, prime minister of Israel

They think they've set the time and date
for Satan to unlock Hell's gate
but the Devil doesn't have to wait
on their permission.
He is himself a head of state
– it's his decision.

They speak so glibly about Hell
and their delusion suits him well
for the Devil's longed since Adam fell
for human fiends
and these men boast his ranks will swell
beyond his dreams.

Soldiers as demons! Do they stop to think?
Worse than machines, they'll never shrink
from any crime, or at the brink
of genocide;
humanity gone out of sync,
dead-eyed.

With Trump and Netanyahu's zeal
everyone loses in this deal.
Armageddon played for real
– and then?
Can zombie armies ever feel
human again?

I am appalled – yet recognise
these awful means are mine – in lies,
contempt and othering. In size
and reach alone they differ.
When I coerce, grudge or despise
then people suffer.

Netanyahu, Trump – this pair
want to be envied for their power
and yet, despite all this, they are
brothers to me.
If I exclude them then I share
their strategy:

their ‘Us-and-Them’, their vile scapegoating
which keeps ‘Us’ pure and ‘Them’ revolting;
that dominance maintained by voting
‘strong’ men in.
Who inflates them – keeps them floating?
The Citizen.

And Hell – it’s not some place apart.
Its gates are in the human heart.
It’s every individual’s part
to wield the key.
Where do Hell and Heaven start?
They start with me.

Source: Al Jazeera on YouTube, 16 February 2025
Video of Benjamin Netanyahu speaking at a press conference alongside Marco Rubio, Secretary of State, United States of America: “We have a common strategy, and we can’t always share the details of this strategy with the public, including when the gates of hell will be opened, as they surely will, if all our hostages are not released, until the last one of them.”

THE NIGHT SKY OVER TEL AVIV
during a bombardment by Iran

At the mosque of Shah Abbas in Isfahan,
in the half-dome ceiling of the porch,
raining towards you, yet arrested, stone
drips and dangles
in a honeycomb of concave niches.

They hang, these turquoise millefiori jewels,
yet each is pointing to its twin above,
and up, and up, to the golden apex,
the source of all this pouring, soaring,
endlessly replenished power.

Trajectories of missile interception
rise to their zenith and expire.
Incoming death burns like a comet
running its finger down
the frail ribbed vaulting of the sky.

Source: BBC 1 News, 13 June 2025

STAYING IN TEHRAN

a poem found within a report, with interviews,
by Siavash Ardalan, BBC Persian Service

Evacuating a city of ten million ...
The roads out of Tehran are choked with traffic ...
... a desperate goodbye ...
One Tehran resident, who wishes to remain anonymous,
told us why he is staying ...

I'm staying in my home.
I'm staying in my city.

I'll try to stick to my routines.
I'll try to find a café that's open and go there.

If I see a couple of people in the street
I'll smile at them – try to lift their spirits.

I'll call my friends more often,
support them, make them feel better.

I think right now we have no one
but each other ...

Source: BBC 1 News At Ten, 17 June 2025
Voiceover in italics
Interview content verbatim

POINT OF VIEW

I am always looking down on these desperate people,
wedged together, thrusting towards food
but here's a photo taken, not of an attention-grabbing scene,
but in a period of waiting
where one woman in the crowd has grown so weary
she's up-turned her empty cooking-pot onto her head,
is trying to rest that double burden on her hand

and it takes me into other stillnesses:
a mother menstruating into sodden clothes – there is no water;
an ancient man wordlessly begging God to let him die;
the dense stench of rubbish, sweet rot of shit,
acrid burning rubber, a heavy veil of gone-rogue chemicals;
the heat in shadeless avenues of rubble,
the hot torpor in the waiting-pens

but still the ocean's busy with the coast, the waves arriving,
leaving, as they always have, along the strand,
and on my radio, the Israeli spokesman must be unaware
his stridency reveals a hidden plea
not to have to live always in that moment
when you see the horizon breaking,
the sea gathering itself up

and I read his president said,
I agree there are many innocent Palestinians ... but
if you have a missile in your goddamn kitchen
and you want to shoot it at me,
am I allowed to defend myself?
That *but*. That knot of shock and grief and flailing.
No bird flying over a tsunami, leaves in its beak.

Photo Credit: AFP/Getty Images Source: *The Guardian*, 22 August 2025
Quotation: Isaac Herzog, president of Israel, interviewed by Rageh Omaar,
ITV International Affairs Analyst, 13 October 2023
Source: ITV News online
3/israeli-president-says-gazans-could-have-risen-up-to-fight-hamas

A PLAN FOR THE DEVELOPMENT OF GAZA

What does the sand feel?
Dumped over bodies hustled into shallow graves,
hurled up to heaven by contemptuous bomb blasts,
blown across bulldozed olive groves,
trampled by a million footsteps
displacing themselves along the Gaza coast,
the sand feels nothing.
It was made to be moved.
Formed from the crushing of large things into small,
it believes that all things will be ground
smaller and smaller till they disappear.

CEASEFIRE

what the Welsh learned from the war between Wales and Ireland

On both sides, we managed to stop the fighting.
We managed to agree that Alder should lead us
– all he needed was time.
We watched him gladly,
our embodied Future Without War
as he moved among us at the celebration.

On our side, we shouldn't have neglected
to win over The Unreconciled One
– implacable he could be,
but surely, we thought, surely ...
He made his move suddenly,
thrusting our young branch head-first into the fire.

Convulsive slaughter,
worse than the worst because hope had gone,
till in all of Ireland
– five pregnant women in a cave,
of the Welsh fighters
– seven bewildered men.

For our remnant – in Harlech, paralysis;
in Gwales, dreaming. Then one of us
opened the door and all we had lost rushed in,
flooding us out, onto the road, with our burden
of wisdom. At the appointed place, we dug it into the ground.
In all generations its testimony flowers.

In *The Mabinogion*, the ancient cycle of Welsh heroic tales, the story, *Branwen, Daughter of Llŷr*, deals with a war between the Welsh and the Irish. A hard-won peace agreement is ruptured by a ruthless yet conflicted Welsh character, bringing both sides to near extinction. A long period of disorientation and recovery follows before the Welsh process the trauma into words.

JOINT ENTERPRISE

Soldiers know
that somewhere
down the road
waits
the awful
juncture
of nail
and flesh:

a fist
full of iron,
the point
on skin,
a hand
full of hammer-shaft,
its hefting,
the terrible
– strike –
the hot gout
flooding the fingers,
the second
blow.

They do
this
for us.
We'd better
be sure
it's what we want;
that it's never
our first,
or futile,
choice;

that we
step out
of the shadows
where we stand
clutching
the bag of nails.

CITIZENS AND POLITICIANS

ASSAULTS ON DEMOCRACY

CAMPAIGNERS FOR VOTER REGISTRATION, MISSISSIPPI

A crucifixion
but the cross is a threatened man.
A bleeding victim clings to him.
In the foreground another sprawls,
nearly dead, trying to rise.

The painter positions us
face on to them
in the final moment
we could intervene
before the irreversible end.

Night in a stony place.
Flaring torches, from the right,
cast into the frame
only the posse's shadows
yet we know these men.

Everything in sepia
except the blood.
Worst of all
is that shadow-infiltrated space
which is the last of safety.

The stalwart man, in profile,
looks across that gap
not in heroic self-assertion but
chin down, with the sombre, measuring regard
a mirror offers to appalling times.

Chaney, a Black local,
and Schwerner and Goodman,
New York Jews, beaten and shot;
Chaney castrated;
Goodman buried alive.

The Deputy Sheriff told the Klan,
You've struck a blow for the White man ...
You've let those agitating outsiders
know where this state stands.
Go home now and forget it.

Those we treat the worst
we loathe the most
because they've seen our ugliest of faces.
The unforgiveable sin.
Nothing's too bad for them.

Source: 'Murder In Mississippi', a painting by Norman Rockwell in *Look* magazine, 29 June 1965, to accompany Charles Morgan's investigative article, 'Southern Justice', about the killing of three civil rights workers in Nashoba County, on 21 June 1964.
Quotation: attributed to Deputy Sheriff, Cecil Ray Price in 'Murder in Mississippi', Howard Ball (University Press of Kansas, 2004)

THE ILLEGAL PROROGATION OF PARLIAMENT, WESTMINSTER

Kabul – that day when the wedding guests exploded;
that other when I let a wee girl on my platform ricochet
from and towards her mother's spew of blame,
or the day when I didn't shelter
a railway worker from a racist shower ...

Some close at hand, some far.
Kabul or Coleraine station, the same acid rain.

That day in Coleraine station when I saw the airiness
its architect had enticed inside and a guard whose smile
kept all our doors ajar, and in the town, a shopfront
of bottles, wittily displayed.
Such things ... light-filled.

These close at hand. In far
Kabul or in Coleraine, the same inherent shine?

Today, when our democracy exploded,
I was tread-milling for an email thrill when I caught
the acrid taste of tipping-point.
In the rank mulch of small misdeeds
the great ones grow

in far Kabul or in Coleraine or Westminster
we choose – violence or light.

On 17 August 2019, 63 people died when an Islamic State suicide bomber attacked a wedding in Kabul.

On 28 August 2019, the British Prime Minister, Conservative leader, Boris Johnson, advised Queen Elizabeth II to prorogue (temporarily suspend) the Westminster parliament.

On 24 September, the Supreme Court ruled this unlawful. Johnson's critics believed the move was an attempt to frustrate parliamentary scrutiny of the final stages leading to Brexit, the withdrawal of the UK from the European Union.

ASSAULTS ON DEMOCRACY, WASHINGTON

Gorse is incognito,
covert, under swags of goose-grass
and drooping blackberry plumes.

In Spring, the fields' flâneur,
a gorgeous braggart
and even now, in grey-green camouflage,

gorse has nurslings,
tender shoot-tips
pliant to the touch.

Well, every assassin blends in with the crowd
and – Winter's confederate, his place-holder
in the hedge – gorse smiles

as it consolidates its vantage-points,
extends its scaffolding
of threat.

On 6 January 2021, supporters of President Donald Trump attacked the United States Capitol in an effort to prevent a stage in the ratification of the election of Democrat presidential candidate, Joe Biden.

COMPASSION

Their sing-along-a-mingling won't spread contamination
nor their consciences weigh heavy in the balance
against their jingling pockets
for don't they have immunity from the herd?

Their bubble floats on seas that sink the rest of us.
Compunction's prick has bounced off that thick skin
for aren't they party people who deserve
their bit of fun?

These sniggerers who pushed us off the raft,
do you think they'd, nonetheless, be capable
of holding out a hand?
You have to hope.

You have to will that no one's ever lost,
that absolutely no one's left behind,
that each of us stays human
or becomes.

Source: 'Partygate', Channel 4, Halcyon Heart Films, a docudrama based on the so-called Partygate illegal gatherings during Covid restrictions, including several in Downing Street, the official residence and office of the British Prime Minister, Boris Johnson. First broadcast on 3 October 2023.

SAVIOUR

He is the other Jesus,
the one who emerges, grinning,
onto the platform beside the governor;
the one who is vindicated
by the mob roaring,
Barrabas! Give us Barabbas!
who is borne aloft on their hands
and passes out of history
into our bloodstream.

Ecce homo, the governor then declares
of the would-be saviour, Jesus
Call-Me-Christ. But he's
 our own fragility embodied
– is it this we hate and want to kill?
Take him away! Take him away!
Yet pity Barabbas, a tough bladder
inflated by our breath, floating forever
on the current of our self-contempt.

Sources: *The Gospel of Mark* 15:6 – 15 The murderous insurrectionist, Barrabas is released from prison at the frenzied crowd's insistence, in preference to Jesus Christ. Some sources give this man's full name as Jesus Barabbas.

Words in italics from *The Gospel of John* 18 & 19. *Ecce homo* 'Behold the man' is said by Pontius Pilate, governor of the Roman province of Judea, inviting the mob to consider that Jesus Christ may be an innocent man.

TERRORISM

The war came to us
while we were idly watching buses shunting between their numbered pens,
as we were bantering in the queues, some youngsters chewing gum
and a man laughing

The war came to us
in a scruffy shopping bag weaving between the café tables

The war came to us
across the farmyard in the darkness, cut the phoneline
and pushed the kitchen door ajar so quietly
we never saw it coming

The war came to us
while we were in the Gospel Hall praising the Lord, our Saviour

The war came to us
in a crowded bar at Hallow E'en,
exhausting a shotgun magazine, reloading,
finishing the job and laughing, *Trick or Treat!*

The war came to us
fearlessly willing to sacrifice the lives of other people

A war came to us
and Sir Patrick Vallance noted in his diary:
PM ... begins to argue for letting it all rip ...
DC says, 'Rishi thinks just let people die and that's okay'...
PM ... back on to ... 'Most people who die have reached their time anyway'.

Sources: Extracts from the diary entry for 25 October 2020 of the British government's chief scientific adviser during the Covid pandemic, Sir Patrick Vallance. See Covid-19 Public Inquiry: Transcript of Module 2 Public Hearing on 20 November 2023.
The Guardian 'Patrick Vallance contradicts Rishi Sunak's evidence to Covid inquiry' by Peter Walker and agencies 20 November 2023 https://www.theguardian.com/uk-news/2023/nov/20/patrick-vallance-contradicts-rishi-sunak-evidence-to-covid-enquiry

PM: British Prime Minister, Boris Johnson;
DC: government adviser, Dominic Cummings
Rishi: Rishi Sunak, Chancellor of the Exchequer

PHOTOGRAPH OF A PARTY LEADER

In some old churches you can find
the letters P A X
set in a circle of thorns.
An image to snag the mind.

And here he is,
bowed down
by too great a weight
– how casually
violence flaunts its potency
by filling yet more graves –
in tears, in need of comfort
from one of the bereaved.

Our representative,
lacerated, always vulnerable,
reaching for peace
through thorns
and not through blood.

P A X - peace (Latin)
Photo Credit: Ann McManus
Source: *The Irish News*, 3 November 1993

John Hume, leader of the Social Democratic and Labour Party, at the burial, on 2 November 1993, of five of the eight victims of a sectarian shooting in The Rising Sun pub in Greysteel, Northern Ireland during a Hallow E'en party on 30 October
This was a reprisal for The Shankill Road Bombing, an IRA attack in Belfast on a Loyalist paramilitary group on 23 October which killed ten and wounded fifty. These resorts to violence nearly derailed negotiation, secret at the time, which eventually led to the Belfast / Good Friday Agreement of 1998.

TO A BELLIGERENT NORTHERN IRISH POLITICIAN

You justify violence
with the ardour of a convert

for you must remember
when we kissed
and were young

how among the bombs
all you wanted
was love.

‘TROUBLES’ JOURNALIST

Scenting the wind, ear cocked
for the tell-tale twig-break
of a swerve away from truth;
remembrancer, nursing the detail
we find so hard to carry;
deft engineer of meaning,
delicately picking from among the facts
this wire, and that; their touch
lightning
that pins us, shadowed or spot-lit.

Stunned, we stumble, but you head on out,
urging us to follow, not to be afraid:
Your wounds – you tell us – those jagged wells ...
don’t cap them, and don’t let them fester
– foul cisterns, poisoning every move.
Go down toward each dark meniscus
in which you see yourself coming to meet you,
because you know,
you know what suffering is
and what the suffering need.

Prompted by ‘Living With Ghosts: The Inside Story of a ‘Troubles’ Mind’
by Northern Irish journalist, Brian Rowan, Merrion Press, 2022

CITY LIGHTS

At night I see how frail the city is
– our brilliancies just feints
to hold at bay the darkness
we have never made our friend

though it's less the dark we fear
than what, or who,
might be approaching
through it.

It is ourselves we dread
– how we can turn and rend the weakest
when we choose to make a midnight
in the soul, switch off the heart.

THE EMERGENCY ULTRASOUND UNIT, CARDIFF

Walking to Emergency Ultrasound
I skirted coloured plastic buckets
beneath drips from punctured ceilings

– *we are beleaguered;*
  like the early stages of a civil war –

yet I was called on time
and treated well and kindly,
the care maintained against the odds

– *my mother* it suddenly came to me
  never felt properly cared for –

her querulousness,
her famished rage and put-downs

were pleas to be loved
enough to make her sure
it was safe to love.

I walked home along the asphalt path
through littered bushes
by the roaring motorway

– *what is unravelling us;*
all of us here?

CITIZENS AND POLITICIANS

CHANGE

SHÏFT

Niver hae A seen tha second whun a sparra, stapt
in its flicht, draps frae tha sky
but A hae fun a wee broon floo'ch,
nae wechtier in ma han nor a see'ch,
an there's me houlin tha en o a wurl.

An thon Rushan peilat – an Icarus
drapt, face doon, tha Febooary snaw
a mither tae him, sheetin his boadie
in a kine beddin, haes he no come
tae tha en o his worl?

Frae furst tha worl begun it haes bin endin,
but noo it's we that ir hanin Daith his ordèrs;
we that wull cast him oot. It's we
wud be Daith
an en tha worl wersels.

floo'ch	ball of fluff or soot
wechtier	heavier
see'ch	a sigh

CHANGE

I've never seen the moment when a sparrow, stopped
in its flight, drops from the sky
but I've bent to lift a puffball of feathers,
earth-coloured, light as a sigh,
and found myself holding the end of a world.

And that Russian pilot – an Icarus
dropped, face down, mothered
by the February snow sheeting him gently,
has he not reached
the end of his world?

Since first the world began it has been ending
but now it's we who thrust on Death his orders;
we who crave his kingdom. We
would be Death
and end the world ourselves.

NEWID

Ni welais erioed yr eiliad pan fo aderyn y to,
wedi'i atal yn ei ehediad, yn syrthio o'r nen
ond rwy wedi codi dwrn o flew'r un lliw â'r ddaear,
mor ysgafn ag ochenaid,
a dyma fi'n dal diwedd byd.

Ac yntau – peilot Rwsia – Icarws
wedi cwympo, wyneb i lawr, a'r eira Chwefror
yn fam iddo, yn gorchuddio ei gorff yn dyner
– onid yw ef wedi dyfod
i ddiwedd ei fyd?

Ers y dechrau, mae'r byd wedi bod ar ddarfod;
ond bellach, ninnau sy'n rhoi i Farwolaeth gorchmynion;
ninnau sy'n dyheu am ei deyrnas.
Marwolaeth mynnwn fod
a diweddu'r byd ein hunain.

PRODUCTIVITY

Maguire's Bay, Ballycastle, Antrim

The many hands of the wind
brush the sea's nap
shoreward, shoreward,
sweeping in as navy,
reversing to an underside of teal
and on again, again,
in the dark blues of a bruise.

This shirring energy is all the wind's,
dashing its impasto down in all directions
on this supple canvas,
setting off explosions underwater
– chrysanthemum fireworks plumping up
into the liquid sky –

and between the shore and skerries
a vast roughland, flexing
in colours of abalone
– those oily iridescences
of eau de nil and indigo, Parma blue,
jade, purple ...

How hard I find it
to let things be
not for
but with
me.

CHOICE

You say *pissoir* and I would have thought
of the dank and secret place
we children used behind the playground
(too far to run home)
but today I think of the heaving sea
outside my window
– blue-green algae in the bay
for the very first time.

You say *pissoir* and I would have thought
of a niche for the neat discharge
of what would be considered
noisome and offensive anywhere else
but now I think of the dream
in which I saw a concentrate of violence
offloaded without shame
in the public square –

people being drowned
in some kind of sewer while a voice said,
Worse than this happens.
You are so naïve.
Yes, the human heart's a sump
and such contempt the scum
brewed from a festering
hatred of ourselves.

You say *pissoir* and I see how things are
and I say the heart's
a green bough too
where a bird might nestle,
and it's a lens,
like a jewel,
letting light in,
refracting it
in colours we hardly know we hold.

BRUTALISTS

Stone
        was nameless
till an eye judged it
makeweight, quern-stone,
threshold, lintel …

        had no desires,
even as it found itself
set up as *idol*,
bloodied as *weapon*;

        obedient,
it held to gravity's law
when it was piled up with intent
to overawe, to subjugate,

        was humble
when claims were made for it
as touchstone for reality
given it's absolutely concrete.

Stone
        simply closed its eyes
and dreamed of how it knows
that mass and weight
are no more real than

        the drift of water,
the feather-shedding snow,
the tiny footsteps
of encroaching ice –

        all the gentlenesses.

INT ÉN BEC

Int én bec
ro léic feit
do rinn guip
glanbuidi
fo-ceird faíd
ós Loch Laíg
lon do craíb
charnbuidi.

Ninth-century Irish
Loch Laíg is Belfast Lough.

THE BLACKBIRD BY BELFAST LOUGH

The wee bird
has wheept from
a beak tip
bright yellow
flings a note
over-lough
black bird – branch
heaped yellow.

thon	that
merle	blackbird
syne	since
bigged	built
thole	endure
mairch	border
blattèrs	pummles
powce	dust

THON MERLE

Thon merle that wheeple’t oot a thoosan yeir lang syne
bes singin noo tae me.

Daes it no see whut we thole here?
Or daes it see an sïng, heedless o whut we dae?

Fur we hae bigged a hoose o pain
in tha gairden we wur gien.

War leps tha mairch, blattèrs tha dure,
pits its coul han on me, on you,

an sens thaim croods frae east an sooth
in hope, or no hope, trevlin

till heich waas bar thaim
an iverie dure slams shut.

Shut in is whut A am,
ma bak tae tha waa, aye brace’t agin ma foes.

Throu some wee neuk but
tha merle’s sang seeples,

lik seeds in simmer air it rises,
lik waftin powce, licht in tha mirk

in spite o tha wuntèr eftèr iverie sprïng
an thon stree’ch o wattër tae tha far lochside.

A see. A see tha jeggèd thoarns
an tha yella cairns o whun.

Aye, merle! A’ll try, lik you,
amang tha baith o thaim tae sïng.

PLEA

Shall I pray to the Sea God, Mannanán Mac Lir?

My kitchen window frames a view to the north-west
out on the Sea of Moyle
where Kenbane, a chalk prow thrusting north-north-east,
butts the horizon, insisting on
the flickering slash on the water
just below the skyline.
It marks the royal precincts of the god,
where his many rooftops puncture
the vast membrane of the sea.

If I were standing on Ceann Bán
– that white headland –
I'd see the ocean churning
from his commerce, stables, cattle
and the to-and-fro at Carraig Mhanainn,
his seat and audience hall.

I can't escape him.
Only the very highest tide brings me a brief respite.
Yet I chose to live here
in sight of the nexus of his powers
and I know he told my ancestors:
Where you see only brine I see
a Plain of Delights, meadows blossoming,
pastureland, forests and mountains,
territories richly peopled ...

so I can't unsee the devastation
caused by our contempt
and the small coin of my activism,
flung in the balance,
can never weigh enough
to tilt it back to true.

From the silver branch of evening,
over Carrick Mannan, the golden apple of the sun
hangs, and droops, and sinks, and disappears.
The sea is lilac, the cloudbanks plum.

My heart, capsizing, steadies.
The god sees differently to us:
my tiniest gift a barb
in the feathers
that tip the scale.

Quotation: from 'Immram Brain' (The Voyage of Bran), 7th- or 8th-century Irish poem

CITIZENS AND POLITICIANS

TACTICAL VOTING

THE TRANSACTIONALIST

If, one day, he were to find himself
in the ditch by the side of Murder Mile,
clothes and money gone, battered,
anonymous as any loser
and see the Good Ol' Boys go by
on the other side

may he come to consciousness
in a stranger's room, in someone else's bed,
between sheets he doesn't own,
with a foreign doctor saying,
to an unfamiliar guy who's leaving,
I'll take care of him. And bill you.

There are other kinds of flensing.
He might halt his motorcade, exit the limo,
drawn to someone in the crowd whose gaze
is breathing his most covert, shameful name
and weighing his despair at how it clings to him
yet who calls out, in front of all the people,

I've been waiting for you!
Spend the day with me.

THEY CAME FOR THE JOURNALISTS

They came for the journalists.
Now we don't know what's going on.
That's what we used to say
but now the journalists are disappeared
simply by denial and a fresher lie.

Don't tell them that the journalists' words
are harboured in our synapses,
messaging, processing and imprinting
a samizdat analysis
that issues in everything we do.

Our real estate is everywhere – open
and impregnable, and though we're certainly afraid,
for the mind is tender,
we're writing something indestructible
– each of us a living word.

Title, and quotation (in italics): an allusion to a poetic paraphrase of sentiments expressed by Martin Niemöller, a German Lutheran pastor and opponent of Nazism: oppressive regimes pick off one group after another unless all groups stand in solidarity.

samizdat: Russian for 'self-published', referring to 'underground' literature dissenting from the political orthodoxy of the former Soviet State

IN THE EYE CLINIC WAITING ROOM, CARDIFF

Broken lock-gates, my irises froze open. Light thundered through.
Straining to resist, they torqued themselves to incandescent pain.
Muscle, after all, these 'windows of the soul',
designed to flex and alter as conditions change.
Immobilised, what could they do but splinter,
beg for night, for shuttering. In vain.
Sentries bleeding, unrelieved.

I thought of Zaporizhzhia, Rafah, Sa'ana, Omdurman,
wherever people brace day after day to live at an extreme,
where they have to feed and work and plan, as though
the times were ordinary, where they have to embody 'sane'
while the body is tortured without a wound,
its signals jammed and over-ridden, twisted to a pitch
that snaps the cells – how can the mind not stagger?

Beneath the headlines, this suffering churns on:
the fear there will be no bread, no medicine, no milk, no mercy,
no one to rely on, no one who cares. I wait
for the specialist's expertise in the Service for the Nation's Health,
a service born from fellowship in pain. Compassion
– here trained, and organised, and brought to bear –
all of us here know this is what heals us. All of us here.

GROUP THINK

They're all the same – one as bad as the other.
A grumble of assent goes round the room;
a general puffing-up of feathers, a strut
of the un-gullible, who see things as they are,
and a bristling power expands itself
from *You only have yourself to count on.*

It isn't that we just don't care
but that we care so much and are so often
disappointed; not that we don't want justice
but we see how things are
and the cynic seems a realist in saying,
Clutch what's your own.

Then a woman ventures, *No. Some politicians*
are decent people, trying to get good things done.
A pause. Then a deflation, and each of us
is standing in the chill
of a world where our only shelter is each other
and the choices ours.

HEALTHCARE, HOUSING, JOBS ...

Every July I took the message from the bonfires on Eleventh Night:
It's you we want to burn.
Next day I'd see the ashes on the pitted asphalt at our terrace-end:
We didn't burn you – this time ...

As a Catholic in the Sixties, I could see that a desire
too terrible to name, too shameful to acknowledge
was enacted through the violence of fire,
was even made respectably desirable

and this year, on the bonfire at Moygashel,
migrants in a boat fare forward through invisible waves,
effigies burning without pain, as though real people
can be burnt alive as easily, as though it's normal, really,

to solve a problem the traditional way
through flames in the darkness with the neighbours cheering,
till a point is reached when the heat takes over
and anything's justified.

We are addicted to the politics of fire.
So simple – it burns everything down
to Us and Them, keeps our politicians tribal,
sends our aspirations up in smoke.

We will always burn – for those we love, and even our hatred
flares because we care so much – but this hot power
can be wrangled into schools, clean water, sewers ... into all the prose
that makes life liveable. This is what politics is for.

Photo Credit: Niall Carson / PA
Source: *The Irish News*, 12 July 2025
Journalist: Mark Robinson
Caption: 'Effigies of migrants in a boat burn atop a bonfire at Moygashel, Co Tyrone, July 12, 2025'

Bonfires are lit every year on the eve of 12 July commemorate the victory of King William III, a Protestant, over King James II, a Catholic, at the Battle of the Boyne in 1690.

TYRANNY

The woodcutter and his child
go hand-in-hand through the forest maze.
The boy sees that the axe-head on his father's shoulder
has his father's mother's eye.
Nestled there, *You'll burn in hell,*
she mouths at her grandson, grinning.
The boy has breakfast bread
turning to crumbs in his grip.

Behind them, the birds are gathering
– so many and with such a sound that his father falters.
We could stop here, the boy says. His father looks away.
The birds flock round them, hungrily.
His father lets the axe-head drop,
scythes his hand along its edge, smears the blade well.
Run away, he urges his son,
then turns back, heavily.

When I hear it said of a man like this,
He was doing the best he could, my heart clenches.
I don't always do *the best*. Neither do you.
So why must it be true of anyone?
That father gave to a tyrant
the loyalty we owe only to love.
Among her implacable trees he longs for accusation,
so his heart can break and call out for his son.

BY ORDINARY MEANS

On the last day of the heatwave
we took the boat to Rathlin,
spent the afternoon soaking up sun
alongside the seals on the foreshore.
Silence
gifted itself like a miracle

and I hadn't known that the sea's a lathe
till I watched it turn, and turn
from its flat, flexing sheet
– right-to-left along its very edge –
a corkscrew shaving of liquid chrome,
a sinuous, silver message, on repeat

and I thought of the painting
where the Archangel Gabriel
– elbows cocked, gorgeous wings
framing his rayonnant halo –
offers the Virgin
God's breath through a mouth organ's lungs.

Prompted by the painting, 'Annunciation With Mouth-Organ'
by Kevin Sinnott

OUR STUBBORN LITTLE ACTS OF LOVE

It's Lucifer who used to bring the dawn
to hilltop, forest, valley, plain and shore.
Light-bearer Devil, brightness putrefied,
envier of innocence, decrier of the second chance,
the cynic's friend, the snuffer-out,
he loves to the hold the mirror up
so we can see our ourselves, sparklers in hand,
the mighty darkness sniggering behind us.

Angel of Light, he chose to be its masterly subverter,
bolstering our misbelief that light and dark are equal
(his great lie) and the victories of darkness always total
whereas he knows the spark zigzagging through the stubble,
or gently spiralling up, can smoulder to a conflagration,
that the tiniest light is never killed but hidden and
burst out it will, so watch him try to dazzle us
with shame at our weakness,
blind us to his own ...

DOMESTIC POLITICS

Held tightly by his mother
the infant tugs her head towards him
so his cheek can nestle against hers,
and he looks up, only at her – his world.

It's nearly a decade since my mother died.
I've kept this icon that was hers
on the high shelf above my desk, a fixture
I wasn't curious about – something no longer seen

but, yesterday, the woman looked at me
– inclined towards her child yet her gaze on me
direct, and sad, and showing me she knows
all that I've done to innocence like his.

How carefully she guards her boy, for now,
from everything she knows he'll come to know,
for all I'll do to him but she
hasn't closed her heart.

Her deep – accepted – sorrow
pools behind her eyes and she reflects on it,
even as she's gazing
compassionately at me.

Nine centuries ago
she was painted in Constantinople.
Sent as a gift to Kyiv, she's in Russia now
and claimed as their patroness.

This Jewish woman, 'Our Lady of Tenderness',
inhabits but transcends our politics,
and lets my mother, tender at last, reach across
the greatest of all borders to embrace me.

THIS, AND THIS TOO

Night. I walk a shred of the Milky Way,
a luminescent path of scattered white.
Like sugar on a slate, the stars' display,
while here pale limestone lays a track of light
along the boreen between hedge and hedge,
a grosser version of the road above.
Brightness from rock: this seems to me a pledge
that nothing is impossible to Love;
and earlier, on the beach, the setting sun
struck swarms of tiny stars from the damp sand.
I walked on constellations as they shone
in a beige sky, a heaven on the strand.
Both these are true: I walk in doubt or dread;
I walk on stars with stars above my head.

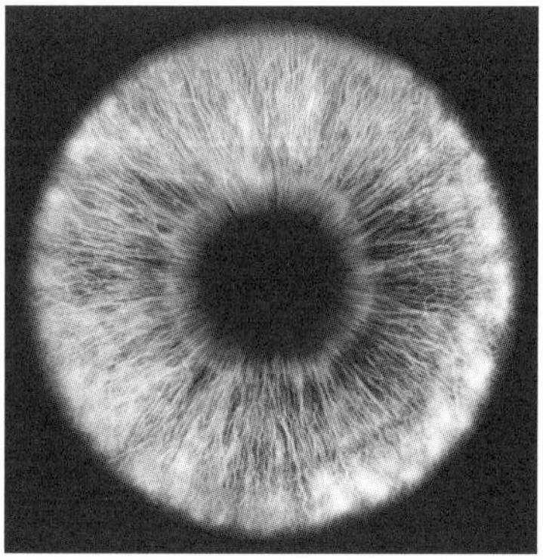